COMING UNDONE

The Love Collection

Volume 1

Nancy Arroyo Ruffin

Copyright © 2015 Nancy Arroyo Ruffin

First Edition Print, January 2015

Coming Undone is published by
CreativeInk Press
Bergenfield, NJ 07621
info@nancyarroyoruffin.com

Cover Design and Concept by
Sal Acosta
s.artist22@yahoo.com
917.774.1320

ISBN: 0692276203
ISBN-13: 978-0692276204

DEDICATION

For every person who has ever loved or longed to be loved and to the man who has shown me what true unconditional love is.

We are never so vulnerable as when we love.
Sigmund Freud

CONTENTS

ACKNOWLEDGMENTS

To experience the kind of soul shifting, transformative love that is documented in this book one must first learn to fall in love with themselves. The road to self-love is long, arduous, and sometimes bumpy. However, without travelling it and re-discovering who we are and learning to love ourselves unconditionally, we cannot openly and honestly love another. I am grateful for all who have crossed my path and through knowing them, have taught me important lessons in life and love. Most importantly, I'd like to acknowledge the man who was my inspiration for this book. Every writer has a muse and he is mine. Thank you to my best friend, my lover, and my life's partner, Lamar, for not only allowing me to love him, but for also loving me exactly as I am.

For a seed to achieve its greatest expression, it must come completely undone. The shell cracks, its insides come out and everything changes. To someone who doesn't understand growth, it would look like complete destruction.

Cynthia Occelli, Resurrecting Venus

Coming Undone

Every night I'd lay my head on his chest,
a synchronized symphony of melodic stillness.
I longed for him the way night yearns for the moon.
I was afraid to love him, but even more afraid not to.
I wanted to asphyxiate in his presence just so that
I could inhale every part of him.

My hands memorized the curve of his lips
and the various incantations he said my name.
I craved the curl of his tongue,
the strength of his back,
the tenderness of his touch.
Even the way we made love was poetic.

Being with him made me forget
every experience that came before him.
This was different. He was different.
He made me want to go to church,
to pray, to thank the Almighty
for deeming me worthy of this experience.
This was the closest I'd ever been to God.

He was Sunday prayers at noon.
He was salvation.

His was the voice I heard in meditation.

He made me feel alive for the very first time in my life.

I gave him my heart knowing that he had the power
to shatter it into a thousand pieces, yet the only thing
more painful would be spending a lifetime
not knowing how great a love like his could be.

Your task is not to seek for love, but merely to seek and find all the barriers within yourself that you have built against it.

Rumi

Broke Wide Open

We kissed and my heart exploded. Sometimes I wanted to cry, other times I wanted to bottle up this moment knowing that I've finally felt this kind of love. The kind that breaks you wide open and tears down every wall you've ever built. The kind that makes you want to die every time that you're together just so you can be reminded of what your soul looks like.

Ode to Bukowski

let me enunciate every word

until love flows from my lips like verse

stillness replaces sound in the presence of God

and on Sunday morning I collect the pieces of you

others have left behind, content with your incompleteness

because wounded birds still sing

and at night the round face of the moon peeks in

you are the man all the others should have been.

Oda a Bukowski

déjame enunciar cada palabra

hasta que el amor fluye de mis labios como verso

quietud reemplaza sonido en la presencia de Dios

y el Domingo por la mañana recojo los pedazos de ti

otros han dejado atrás, contenta con su incompletitud

porque los pájaros heridos todavía cantan

y por la noche la care de la luna se asoma

tu eres el hombre que todos los demás deberían haber sido.

Chemistry

we were crazy love
high speed,   better than
drug induced euphoria

reverse chemistry

to avoid explosion
save hearts
because we need those

Química

estábamos loco del amor
velocidad alta, mas mejor que
euforia inducida por fármacos

    química inversa

para evitar la explosión
salvamos corazones
porque los necesitamos

S o, I love you because the entire universe conspired to
help me find you.
Paulo Coelho, The Alchemist

Jupiter

when breath escapes mouth like night

when eyes refuse sleep like death

when every vision is sullied with lust

when my name is the only word your lips will speak

when every lover wears my face

when hands knead blood into skin,

making carnage out of flesh

Ganymede will unbind itself from Jupiter

and you will wonder why you chased the moon

when you already had the sun.

God/Less

Mother warned me about men like you

who steal tongues like ghosts

collecting bones underneath the moon

the clock reads 11:57 pm

and she blames night on these indiscretions

she prays a novena for my broken heart

but I found God on your skin

and that was the only salvation I needed.

God/Less

Mi madre me advirtió sobre los hombres como tu

los que roban lenguas como fantasmas

recogiendo huesos debajo la luna

el reloj marca las 11:57 pm

y ella da la culpa a la noche por estas indiscreciones

ella reza una novena por mi pobre corazón

pero yo encontré a Dios sobre su piel

y esa era la única salvación que necesitaba.

Soul-Mates

Love is the unexpected transformation that occurs when the souls of two people connect. We will spend years searching, connecting, and unravelling until we find the one who will unlock every part of us that has been hidden to everyone else. When that happens we will stand naked, raw, flaws exposed and in our scars they will only see our beauty.

The Alchemist

My teeth clench flesh
shameless and sacrificial.
I always knew you would come
to reclaim what the others
so easily discarded.

I am magnificent magic maker,
melt into my frame like alchemy.

Forever a shadow seeking yours, yet you prefer to hide
and like the Romans, you too shall fall.
For the taste of my thigh still lingers
in the back of your throat.

That thing called love

the more you try to forget

the more you remember

that's the thing with love

even after it's over

it never really leaves you

Portraits

I watched you this morning while you were sleeping. The stillness of your body interrupted only by the peaceful humming of your breath. The faint light of the street lamp absorbed the darkening room and illuminated your skin, highlighting the birthmark on your collarbone. I fell in love with you at that moment. Every time I look at you feels like the first time, like snapping pictures so I could cherish the moments forever.

You swallowed everything, like distance, like the sea, like time. This was my destiny and it was the voyage of my longing, in it my longing fell, in you everything sank.

Pablo Neruda

A poem for Neruda

here I am
in the same place
we first found each other

I wait for you by the shoreline
the seagulls no longer fly
and I wonder if you still think of me

I want to revisit all the moments we spent together,

a cup of coffee at dawn,
the pull of your lips as you inhale your cigarette
the quietude of your voice
the gleam of light that sparkled in your eye the first time
I tasted your skin

in you I wanted to die one thousand deaths
just so I could feel God one more time
always one more time.

Pa' Neruda

aquí estoy
en el mismo lugar
que nos primero encontramos

te espero por la costa
las gaviotas ya no vuelan
y me pregunto si todavía piensas de mí

quiero volver a visitar todos los momentos
que pasamos juntos

una taza de café en la madrugada,
el tirón de sus labios al inhalar su cigarrillo
la tranquilidad de su voz
el brillo de la luz que rebotó en su ojo la primera vez
que probé su piel

en ti me quería morir mil muertes
sólo para poder sentir a Dios una vez más
siempre una vez más.

S he who has never loved or allowed herself to be loved dies the slowest death. It is into love that we are born and reborn. Every time we love we give ourselves permission to begin again.

Drown

verb \ *draʊn* \ : *to die by being underwater too long and unable to breathe*

I used to sit beneath tangerine skies
praying for flowers in December
trapped between zenith and twilight,
unearthing heart from flesh

I try to forget you
delete time from memory, but night still comes
even when I don't want her to.

Ravenous and hungry
I remember your shadow, and the muted
silence of your goodbye

In my stillness we are one
you are the sun, the stars, and the sand beneath my feet
I rest my head on your side of the bed
you were the ocean and I let you swallow me whole.

When night falls

I remember the curve of your tongue
the feel of you; the pulsating beat of our hearts
like cadent rhythm or legato
tied together, our bodies connected
curled into each other like calligraphy.
Synchronicity like church bells at noon.
Sunday spirituals, you are gospel
like alpha and omega.

Sing me a song while my hands
study the arch in your back
the quiver in your lip
the softness of your voice
your scent singed on flesh
like branded cattle
and nightfall refuses to cast
its shadow on your skin.

So I gather up what is left of you
because broken mirrors still reflect light.
You're raw and beautiful like Parisian street art.
An old lady bathes under the moonlight and all I remember
is how bare feet against cobbled stoned roads
always leads back to you.

War Zone

Tell me about every lover you've ever had. Tell me of the first time you felt bones shift underneath epidermis or how fingers dismantled clenched thighs. Tell me about the assembly line of hearts that fell at your feet upon your touch. Recount the first time my scent left you breathless, gasping for oxygen in my embrace. You found me on the other side of paradise, mouth shrouded in defiance. Predatory beast unearthing skeletons of the dead. You didn't think you could love me, did you? Yet, here you are thrusting yourself directly into the line of fire.

Love is a temporary madness, it erupts like volcanoes and then subsides. And when it subsides, you have to make a decision. You have to work out whether your roots have so entwined together that it is inconceivable that you should ever part. Because this is what love is. Love is not breathlessness, it is not excitement, it is not the promulgation of promises of eternal passion, it is not the desire to mate every second minute of the day, it is not lying awake at night imagining that he is kissing every cranny of your body. That is just being "in love", which any fool can do. Love itself is what is left over when being in love has burned away, and this is both an art and a fortunate accident.

Louis de Bernières, Captain Corelli's Mandolin

Mosaic

Love me in hues
beneath sienna suns
until my soul is ablaze
with golden sparks of the Brooklyn Bridge

Love me in black and white
on ebony soil that coils like a rose beneath your touch

Love me with everything you've got
till your bones ache with the memory of me

Recite me a psalm along the East River

Love me without reservation
or fears, or doubts.

Gift me a mosaic of soul shifting love making
and make me forget every lover
that came before you.

The Wanderer

We fell in love along the Nile River
ruthless rebel, savagely excavating frames from bodies

I couldn't tame you
you weren't meant for domestication.

Instead you meander
in search for what belongs to you

I still remember the first time we made love

and the way my body betrayed me
in your presence

in the house of my father I wait for your return

to breathe life back into volcanoes
that have erupted once too many times

reconstruct cells till I'm no longer flawed

rebuild foundations cemented in matrimony

you place your heart in my hand
crown me Queen

and remind me that this is home.

Souls are married long before they meet. It is in the searching where we discover that what we have spent our whole lives seeking has also been seeking us.

Yesterday

we talked about the places we would visit before life got in the way. Strawberry skies, indigo backdrops. The walls wet with sweat. Enamored with the sweetness of quenepas on your lips, the Caribbean breeze sneaks in through an open window. *Eres bella querida*, you whispered. A wisp of hair behind my ear, your breath on my neck and the promise of forever in your eyes.

T herefore a man shall leave his father and mother and hold fast to his wife, and the two shall become one flesh.- Ephesians 5:31

I Do

I fell asleep in your embrace
our bodies entwined
by the divine silence of familiarity
two figures linked by love
and by the thousands of words
we no longer had to speak
The radio plays a bolero
Years of memories
flashback in milliseconds

strangers
friends
lovers
horse drawn carriages
white dresses
the promise of a new day

In you I found shelter
suburban landscapes
picket fences
hot summer days
long wintery nights
baby cries
dreams realized
we redefined forever
the day we said I do.

New Year's Eve

Let's toast at midnight
celebrate the magic of a new year
soak into my skin
feel the fireworks rise inside me.

Collect rainstorms along the Euphrates
wash away the taste of past lovers,
the lips you've devoured,
and bodies you've consumed.

Forget all who tried to break you
they were preparing you for me.

Let me repair your damaged heart
cup your face in my hands
plant roots on soil coveted by Gods
establish our existence in this life and the next.

Show you that this is home
let me fill you with light
so that you never lose your way.

L et her be as the loving hind and pleasant roe; let her breasts satisfy you at all times; and be you ravished always with her love. Proverbs 5:19 (KJV)

C omo cierva amada y graciosa corza, Sus pechos te satisfagan en todo tiempo; Y en su amor recréate siempre. Proverbios 5:19 (KJV)

Free

For a long time, the cycles of the moon left no trace on me. The seasons had no meaning and I was a long way gone. I found comfort in my loneliness and was unaware of my unraveling. Love left me years ago so I didn't recognize you when you arrived; patient and accepting. You loved me in ways I couldn't understand, wholly, and in a language that I wanted to become fluent it. There were parts of me I never knew existed, we were both beguiled by the weight of the moment and our will to never let it go.

Nymph

Someone once asked me what love feels like.

All I could compare it to was a spiritual unfolding;

and the soothing calmness of your breath

on the flesh below my navel.

Life is too short to leave important words unsaid.
I love you. It's that simple and that complicated.

L a vida es demasiado corta para dejar palabras importantes sin decir. Te amo. Es así de simple y así de complicado.

What is love

Love is shedding all the layers that for so long protect us from ourselves. It is being pulled apart at the seams and exposing the parts we believe are too ugly, too complicated, too shameful. The act of love forces us to look past the exterior. It forces us to strip down and look not only at our partners, but also at ourselves. It is our unravelling and when we really look at ourselves, we give others permission to look at us too.

Island love

You are one million candles that light the beach at Boquerón
Even in Aguadilla hearing the coqui's cry, I long for you.
The zephyr carries your scent
and love hides inside palm trees.

You are rose and thorn
sin and salvation
nightfall and sunrise.
You are the pull of the moon
and the erupting force of volcanoes.

In the distance I hear your voice

We are harmony,
so these moments of rhythm and bass
give life to the symphony on your lips.
Our bodies move to the tribal beats of our ancestors.
I revel in your rapture
for I have forsaken a thousand half loves
just to see the light of a new day
dance upon your face.

I used to pray at the catacombs
offering my heart to the Gods.
Now I pray to you and offer you
my longing.

When I had given up on love the Universe whispered in my ear, "not yet". Years later you arrived and I realized that every love until that point was preparing me for you.

C uando yo deje de creer en el amor el Universo
sussuro en mi oido,"todavía no". Años despues, tu
llegaste y en ese momento me di cuenta que
todos los amantes del pasados me estaban
preparando para ti.

Decree

You once asked me why I love you

I replied, *I love you because I know nothing else*
I love you because it is what God has called me to do

You are the moon
and I am the ocean who beckons at your command.
So the question isn't why I love you,
but instead how could I not?

Decreto

Una vez me preguntaste por qué te amo

Yo le respondí:
Te amo porque no sé nada más
Te amo porque es lo que Dios me ha llamado a hacer

Tú eres la luna
y yo soy el océano
que hace señas a sus órdenes.
Así, que la pregunta no es por qué te amo,
sino ¿cómo no?

Becoming Love

My parched lips
long for the sweetness of you
and the endless rhythm of the sea.
Ritualistic acts created by your presence
I bathe myself in new beginnings.

My heart tugs strings
weaving back together
the pieces of my spirit
others frivolously played with.

Intricate tapestries peek through the veil of my truth
reminding me of what real love feels like.

Once dried up inside I am reborn an oasis
rising from sandy wasteland created to quench
the thirst of 1 million skies.

Cleanse me with daily gratitude,
trust, patience, fruitfulness, and love.
For your rippled waves
have awakened dormant dreams
that once flowed through me
like the great river in Egypt.

Through parted waters

and into the desert of infancy

I found myself again.

I valued myself again.

I loved myself again.

and because I love myself

I can now love you

wholly, completely, and honestly.

B e so lost in me that when you look at me you see
yourself.

One

Ours

was

an

unbridled

love

affair.

Inverted

vertebrae

against

bare

wall.

Tongue

on

skin.

Clenched

teeth.

Your

mouth

in

places

I

never

knew

I

had.

Your

scent

familiar

like

the

sound

of

my

own

name.

Your

hands

recognize

the

map

of

my

bones

as

if

they

were

your

own.

And

I

still

remember

the

first

time

you

said

"I love you"

muted

whisper

in

a

crowded

room

and

in

that

moment we finally became one.

You were the treasure longing to be unearthed.

Poetry

Come with me to the cemetery
> let's kneel at the tombs of Hafiz and Shakespeare
>> absolve ourselves in their presence.

Tell me of all the ways you will love me.

>> Stir my colors into earth
> and sow seeds of appreciation for this love.

>> Revel in my complexity.

Study me in ways the others have failed to learn.
Taste me, even when your palette murmurs *enough.*
> Know that when you lay with me at night
> there's more to want here than mere flesh.

And when the moon swallows the night
> place your finger upon brow, mold me into memory
> and drink me till you overflow with verse.

UnSaid

Life is short
memory is long
and there is no greater
regret than words left unsaid.

What you gave me

In your absence
I cannot think
of loving you
without smiling.
What I would give,
to be covered in your fragrance
absorbed in the bigness of you
just once more and say,
I still love you.

It's been almost two decades,
youth has been replaced with age
and reminders of the way you looked at me
still have me enamored.
Let's go back to the beach of Boquerón
and watch the seagulls kiss the sky.

For just one night,
let me see the passion in your eyes,
the touch of your lips
the love residing on your fingertips
and everything else you gave me,
before the island breeze blew in,
and stole your heart away.

Oh, what I would give to
lay beside you,
sleep naked in your bed,
Fill your room
with laughter
and lust,
and the sounds of a new born baby.

We parted ways
travelled different roads

found new loves,
took some into my bed,
and others into my heart.

But you know, as do I
This wasn't always possible.
I didn't always have the desire-
or the courage
to be free,
to be loyal,
to give my heart,
to love so deeply.

These were all your gifts--
To me.

Someday-
When breath escapes me for the last time
I will close my eyes and recollect the first time
love left me breathless
and as I beg the Almighty for forgiveness
I will return to you
hold you in my embrace,
kiss you,
And say,
"I still love you."

L ove is the source of all that lives, all that dies, and all that is eternal.

E l amor es la fuente de todo lo que vive , de todo lo que muere, y todo que es eterno .

Waiting to exhale

You
were
the
poem
lodged
in
my
throat

upon
your
arrival

I
remembered
what
it
felt
like
to
breathe

L ove is wanting to wake up beside you for the rest of our days.

Sunday Mornings

On Sunday mornings
I listen to trumpets playing in the distance
each note proclaims its home on your naked frame
I lay in envy searching the horizon for answers
I can still taste her on your lips

        she broke your heart, you said
        this is the last time, you said

so I welcomed you home
an aubade self-contained in rhyme,
encased between rib and spine.
I walked across each vertebrae
so you could feel the Universe
upon your back.
Knelt in prayer
to the paradise
beneath your feet.
Showed you how
to manifest light from darkness
because morning always approaches.
But tonight, I will revel in the twilight
on the other side of the rainbow
because you are here now
and this moment is all we have.

L ove is everything. It's the only thing. Be blessed in love, always.

E ven at my darkest, you saw my light. You broke down the walls, filled me with love, and let me shine.

E n mi más oscuro, viste mi luz. Usted rompió por las paredes, me llenaste de amor, y me dejaste brillar

Love is patient, love is kind. It does not envy, it does not boast, it is not proud. It does not dishonor others, it is not self-seeking, it is not easily angered, it keeps no record of wrongs. Love does not delight in evil but rejoices with the truth. It always protects, always trusts, always hopes, always perseveres.

Corinthians 13:4-7

Corinthians

The older you get
the more you realize
what love is
and what it isn't.

It isn't about what they can buy you
or where they can take you
or what they can do for you.

It's about who they inspire you to be.
It's about the beauty they see
when you're at your worst.
It's seeing your scars
and wanting to help heal them.

Love makes you feel
like you are the cosmos.
The sun, air, moon, stars
pale in your presence
and to be in the presence of love
is to be in the presence of God.

Communion

You put your hand on my thigh
to soothe my edacious need to
consume the parts of you
that have been hidden in flesh.

I count the hours between dusk and sunrise
memorizing the sentient ravenous dance
of your palm upon my breast
and the way my hip bends to your touch.

In you I lose myself and find myself
all at once.

Every time we make love,
we are giving life to all that exists.
In that sense it becomes communion.
In that sense this love is my sacrament.

Testimony

I never wanted

    to be saved

        just loved in ways

            that would make

                the Gods jealous.

And now these three remain: faith, hope and love. But the greatest of these is love. –Corinthians 13:13

A Note From The Author

Love is the greatest thing one can ever experience. True meaningful love will fill you up with beauty, grace, admiration, acceptance, patience, kindness, and thoughtfulness. This kind of love requires work, commitment, and dedication from both parties, but it is possible to attain. This book was my love letter to my beloved. I have included the following journal pages so that you can begin to document your own love story. If you haven't found your love yet trust that they're out there. He/She is also seeking you just be patient. When the time is right and the stars align the Universe will bring the two of you together.

Coming Undone

The Journal

Above all, love each other deeply.

Date _____

Date _____

Date _____

Date _____

Date _____

Date _____

Date _____

Date _____

Date _____

Date _____

Date _____

Date _____

Date _____

Date _____

Date _____

Date _____

Date _____

Date _____

Date _____

Date _____

Date _____

Date _____

Date _____

Date _____

Date _____

Date _____

Date _____

Date _____

ABOUT THE AUTHOR

Nancy Arroyo Ruffin is an award winning author, poet, and public speaker. Her book Letters to My Daughter was a 2014 International Latino Book Award Finalist for Best Poetry Book. Nancy is the CEO and founder of the women's organization Power of the FIERCE Woman™ and also serves on the Board of Directors for the Where I'm From Foundation for the Arts. Coming Undone is Nancy's third collection of poetry. She currently resides in Bergenfield, NJ with her husband and their daughter.

To connect with Nancy find her on:

Facebook: NancyArroyoRuffin
Instagram: @MsNancyRuffin
Twitter: @MsNancyRuffin
Tumblr: @MsNancyRuffin

Website: www.nancyarroyoruffin.com

Bookings or media inquiries email: info@nancyarroyoruffin.com